THE NEW WORK-LIFE BALANCE

THE NEW WORK-LIFE BALANCE

LEONARD CRIMSON

CONTENTS

1	Introduction	1
2	Historical Context of Work-Life Balance	3
3	Advantages and Challenges of Remote Work	5
4	Strategies for Achieving Work-Life Balance in a Re	9
5	The Role of Technology in Facilitating Work-Life B	11
6	Mental Health and Wellbeing in Remote Work	15
7	Impacts of Work-Life Balance on Job Satisfaction a	19
8	Case Studies of Successful Work-Life Balance Imple	23
9	Future Trends and Predictions in Remote Work	25
10	Conclusion	27

Copyright © 2024 by Leonard Crimson
All rights reserved. No part of this book may be reproduced in any manner whatsoever without written permission except in the case of brief quotations embodied in critical articles and reviews.
First Printing, 2024

CHAPTER 1

Introduction

The very notion of work-life balance has evolved. When you are working from home, your work life and your personal life are no longer separate; each impacts the other in new ways. The organizations that can help their people navigate these complex interconnections will be the ones that succeed—through their exceptional work environment and through the outcomes they deliver. At the heart of the many shifting variables is perhaps the most delicate and important fact of all: employees' relationships with their employers are being tested. Heads of human resources and senior leaders across the organization can use this moment to build and cement that trust, and indeed to deepen the sense of belonging, purpose, and pride. In this article, we will outline some of the biggest challenges and opportunities involved in sustaining remote work.

Our work and work lives have undergone profound changes in this remote era, with long-term implications that we are only just beginning to understand. Overnight, we had to figure out how to keep our teams focused and motivated, how to manage and develop employees when we weren't in the office, how to maintain a company culture, and much more. But one of the biggest shifts—undoubtedly one of the toughest to manage—was the rapid switch to working remotely. At first, we thought this was a huge, temporary experiment, but it has become clear that remote work is here to stay. It may not be forever, and it will not be for everyone, but it will continue to be a big part of our workforce's reality. We are still in the early stages of these changes, but the insights and solutions we have had to learn along the way are invaluable.

Definition of Work-Life Balance

In the past, work and private life were seen as competing separate life spheres, whereby time and energy spent in one sphere (e.g. work) resulted in a reduction of time and energy for the other (e.g. personal life). More recently, work-family directions contend that work and family life are interdependent, and that achievement at one enhances outcomes at the other. Thus, a person with a high level of work-life balance is said to effectively balance between work and personal life, resulting in workers who are satisfied in both life domains. If you feel engaged and fulfilled when you are at work and when you are at home, you have work-life balance.

The work-life balance definition has been difficult to give, but it is often defined as the harmonizing of work and personal life, which can be extremely challenging for many people. Achieving this balance is even more demanding for women, who are often primary caretakers in the home. Both organizations and workers are looking for ways to make the process of integrating job requirements with private life easier. These challenges have been made difficult by the introduction of information technology tools, which have modernized work processes. Workers can now work at any time and at any place, thus considerably reducing temporal and spatial limits on their work.

CHAPTER 2

Historical Context of Work-Life Balance

With the formation of factory jobs and the accompanying pulling of work out of the home, the situation shifted a little bit for a large segment of the population, but people who lived on farms continued to work virtually around the clock, with only seasonal variations in peak workloads. While factory jobs hammered a wedge between work and home, factories still wanted their workers to put in long hours. These long hours trapped parents and children alike. Society responded with some attempts to regulate working hours, and in spite of the image of the 19th century robber baron, even factory workers worked far fewer hours than we are used to in the 21st century. After all, exhausting workers meant that employers could neither extract reasonable work nor sell more products. But the notion of work overwhelming the rest of life was generally accepted as a given.

As recently as just a few decades ago, the concept of work-life balance was virtually completely foreign to most people. The concept has only existed for a short time historically and is a direct product of the radical shift that has recently happened in society's relationship to work. When people in the industrialized world were almost all farmers, work and life were nearly indistinguishable. Home was where productivity happened. Women's work and men's work were less strictly delineated, but they both certainly happened at home and in the fields. If the work was not being done in the fields and homes, it meant that starvation was not far away.

Pre-Remote Work Era

Leaders at these organizations are on record as loving and advocating for the benefits of remote work. Fueled by the successes of these pioneers, other organizations became more open to allowing some employees to work remotely. Tools, services, and communities that support remote work also began to grow. For example, companies like Atlassian resulted in a lot of professional growth and job security for many individuals. In addition, remote work allowed employers to access talent pools and reduce recruiting, facility, and turnover costs. And it provided everyone with more schedule flexibility, time to explore personal interests, and time with friends and families. With all of these benefits more visible to more people, remote work became even more popular!

Before remote work was widely adopted, most employees commuted to an office each day, worked an eight or nine-hour shift, and primarily communicated in person and over company networks. They often didn't work on weekends or once they left the office in the evenings. Many remote workers also performed subcontracting work instead of managing large teams at their employers' companies. Notable organizations worked this way. For example, the fully remote work era. In recent years, a variety of influential organizations transitioned to a remote work structure and showed how productive and meaningful entirely remote organizations could be. Employees at these companies lived in all different countries and time zones.

CHAPTER 3

Advantages and Challenges of Remote Work

Of course, there are disadvantages as well. First, weaker social connections come with the territory. Remote work requires additional effort to support a strong company culture. Therefore, it's important to put in effort to make sure that all employees feel connected and understand the company mission, strategy, and policies. Another potential drawback is that the line between work and personal life can blur. That can lead to employee burnout and reduced well-being. It's important to know whether people are enjoying their remote work or suffering under the burden of it. Regular exposure to managers can help them to assess this.

Under this arrangement, it can be easier to keep the best employees, who can maintain their jobs from anywhere that they choose to live. And where people choose to live is also relevant. The idea of living in an expensive urban area, such as San Francisco, can be unsettling. Many workers might appreciate the opportunity to live somewhere with a lower cost of living. With remote work, that can become a possibility. This can also benefit employers, who in urban areas have previously been paying higher salaries for their employees to live nearby. Those costs can come down considerably.

One of the great advantages of working remotely is that a person's physical location can become less relevant. Indeed, anywhere someone has a stable internet connection, they can get their work done. This fact can have enormous benefits for employers. Perhaps the most obvious advantage is that the universe of potential applicants increases dramatically. Now, a small business can dip into a larger pool of potential employees from a wider range of backgrounds.

Advantages of Remote Work

For employees, remote work means autonomy and flexibility, which are crucial elements in the empowerment of people at work. Remote work implies a better work-life balance, less work-family conflict, and a reduction in work-related commuting stress. Hence, remote work can have a positive impact on an employee's private life because productivity depends on personal well-being. The most immediate reduction is related to the time spent on the home-to-CPOW and CPOW-to-home journey. The time saved is perceived by workers as time invested in personal care, social activities, physical fitness, rest, or eating. This accomplishment results in improved job satisfaction, a strengthened professional identity, and a more stable family life. On a larger scale, it contributes to a decreased congestion pressure within urban areas and a fall in energy consumption.

Remote work, also known as virtual work, telecommuting, or teleworking, is a work arrangement in which employees do not commute or travel from their homes to a central place of work (CPOW) such as an office building, warehouse, or store. More broadly defined, remote work is any form of employment that is performed either partly or entirely from outside of an employer's premises. This workforce management option represents an opportunity for employers to improve work-life balance, employee engagement, talent retention, and productivity. Currently, remote work is made possible by a combination of information and communication technology tools and the many job descriptions that entail desk-based tasks. According to Global Workplace Analytics, the remote worker population could reach 25% of the national workforce by 2020.

Challenges of Remote Work

Work flexibility is a matter of opposition, with one group of employees noting it as the most important attribute in their work, while another group see lack of flexibility or benefits of working with colleagues as reasons to oppose it.

Remote work becomes unproductive when employees are left wandering around aimlessly, unclear of what they are supposed to accomplish in their job. Almost 30 percent of HR leaders believe employees struggle with a clear job purpose when working remotely. Communication is, of course, necessary to clarify expectations and deliverables. However, while remote work tools make communication with remote workers easier, many employees struggle with the desire for synchronous communication. HR leaders consistently cite lack of communication (21 percent) as the second biggest remote work barrier to addressing their remote work challenges.

As the workforce becomes more delineated from the office, both corporate and communal amenities and the vibrant, creative "density" that cities offer may also suffer. Moreover, without the information or impetus that proximity with colleagues creates, remote workers are more likely to become isolated and less likely to contribute to decision-making or innovation. HR leaders feel that social isolation and lack of relationship-building with colleagues is the top challenge of remote work. In a May survey, 80 percent of HR leaders expressed concerns about it.

The move to remote work is not without its challenges. Isolation, lack of purpose, communication difficulties, and burnout are all vices related to remote work. Employers must recognize these challenges and work to mitigate them to ensure that remote work remains a desired work model for those who feel it enhances their lives and work.

CHAPTER 4

Strategies for Achieving Work-Life Balance in a Re

Creating boundaries between work and home life is crucial for everyone in your household. Work together to establish when your work hours start and end. If you have children, this could mean that you are their virtual teacher, provide needed entertainment, prepare meals, and help with chores only when you're on break. Creating a routine based on your work and personal life will contribute to a positive work-life balance. It's especially important to schedule activities that help you mentally transition from work time to personal time. Consider activities such as going for a walk, preparing dinner, or spending time with a loved one.

Have in mind that during periods of uncertainty our productivity might suffer. Many people reacted quite well in the beginning, but then the feelings of loss and grief rushed in. Even the most experienced remote workers struggle from time to time with remote work symptoms, especially loneliness. Developing social connections outside of work can help combat the negative effects of loneliness and provide a greater sense of balance in your life. Try to find time to hang out with family and friends virtually, but pay attention to maintaining social connections. It is much better to work when you're focused and content than when you're stressed or in crisis.

Setting Boundaries

How can you establish required limits and unplug after a workday when you may not even have a workday in the traditional sense anymore? What about your kids, pets, and partner who so far have been respectful of your professional time outside the home? In our view as coaches, the answer to all these questions is an even more disciplined approach to remote work, not dismissal of its power in saving commuting time and searching for your favorite co-workers over rows of half-height cubicles. You need to look for and find new structures that do not necessarily mirror traditional blocks of work time and break time.

As with any way you work, if you want to ensure maximum success and productivity, you need to carefully define expectations for yourself and others. You need to establish new, clear boundaries around work demands and transitions. Though you may still be working in your home, you may not be alone in it, and if you are, blending your private and work life simply will not work. Without external signs like your walk to the car, your subway ride, or drive to the office, role and emotional shifts and physical transitions are more crucial than ever.

CHAPTER 5

The Role of Technology in Facilitating Work-Life B

Companies with flexible and work from home policies rely heavily on trust. Leaders trust that employees are focused on work and making the best use of their work hours. Employees, on the other hand, give the best of themselves trusting that their work will be recognized. The ability to trust employees, and employees to trust their employers, sets the top companies apart. This mutual trust is fundamental to the success of flexible working as the company allows the team to balance their work and personal hours, and in return, employees are committed to ensuring that the projects are progressing. This trust cannot be maintained by monitoring work hours and keystrokes. Some companies, for example, use video surveillance in meetings and even keyboard shortcuts to monitor employee activity. However, the use of these tools can lead some employees to believe that the company trusts them less autonomously and, as a result, stigmatize them, which may not necessarily be true.

- Policies (and execution) based on trust, not surveillance. - Redefining productivity and value with asynchronous and autonomous work. - Fostering inclusion and reducing the sense of isolation. - Supporting the career path and talent development without bias.

Given the importance of achieving work-life balance, business owners and managers have a responsibility to provide the tools and resources that enable each employee to manage their work according to their personal and family needs without suffering negative consequences, and instead thrive at work and in life. With technology playing a central role in remote work facilitation, it is only fitting to explore how tech tools can help team leaders foster not only project progress but also personal well-being. Here are some critical roles fulfilled by technology today:

Productivity Tools

Digital Well-being Tools: The Digital Wellbeing feature in some versions of the Android operating system was created to help people manage screen time and can be especially popular on smartphones used intensively by remote working HR professionals. With it, an HR person could oversee their own personal time goals, set appropriate boundaries, limit notifications, and use focus mode to reduce distractions while trying to focus. The apps allow them to work smarter and to the best of their abilities, and to ensure that sustained high performance is not at the expense of unhindered physical, mental, and emotional time and space to live their lives. Quality HR roles require people to think carefully in pressure-crucially, these apps mitigate the risks of burnout and an eventual loss of professional purpose as pressures accumulate.

Self-Control Apps: Concentration is a prerequisite for effectiveness, and nothing can be more distracting for an HR person on remote work than being continuously drawn to screens displaying incoming emails, chat messages, news feeds, app notifications, and various media posts while actually needing to complete a task offline. There are a number of self-control apps to help maintain high levels of focus over the course of a workday. The premise behind these apps is simple: they control user access to the online experience and give a person the opportunity to concentrate on completing important tasks. Focus – Pomodoro app, with time management technique, and Forest: Stay Focused, Keep Growing, which both gamify concentrating on a task, are useful examples. The apps help people to work without distractions for 25 minutes and, then after a short break, focus on another task for 25 minutes. No barriers to access will prevent them from completing their task immediately. These are particularly useful tools for online facilitation of remote meetings where maintaining team attention is critical, and it is important to have every team member present and focused on follow-on tasks. They free up HR professionals to manage multiple work streams via home-based remote working which, for many, has lost its quiet appeal due to the pull of family members or lonely pets, and a new but unrelated need to check the fridge.

With remote working, the shift to global teams, and the growing need for 24/7 responsiveness, work now reaches into virtual worlds created by digital tools. Purposeful technology use delimits these virtual worlds and can create efficient, focused, and disciplined work. Here are some tools that can help HR professionals maintain or rebuild effective work routines while stabilizing and bringing to balance their work-life world.

CHAPTER 6

Mental Health and Wellbeing in Remote Work

Worker burnout levels have significantly increased over the past year, closely following working hours. Pre-pandemic, the U.S. Bureau of Labor Statistics reported that 3.4% of workers were working remotely. It increased to 42% during the pandemic. It went down to 35% in May 2021, and 20% in September 2021. The return to work really hasn't happened. While things may look promising compared to January 2021, in September 2021, the number of remote workers is still double what it was before March 2020. Contemplating the future, the best thing to do is worry at what point in time we ought to abandon our emotions as we have understood perfectly we are just looking in the dark. Working from home or any other place remote from the employer has become a choice, a right, and is no longer an extension of office hours that fades from sight after remote working, without any chance of exploring the boundaries between the two times and places.

Remote working can have a range of benefits, but it's not without its disadvantages, and for some people, the negative aspects can far outweigh the good. More than two-thirds of professionals reported that they are experiencing worse mental health issues now compared to the start of the pandemic, including 57% who are experiencing burnout from their jobs. One in every three professionals said they think about their job and work projects during their free time. Nearly half of workers and over half of those managing them reported working all, or at least a part, of the weekend for the job. Even when we're not working, we feel as though we are – because our work devices and the software we use are designed for remote work.

Common Mental Health Challenges

Remote work challenges the current dominant narrative which sees dividing up work and private life as unrelated issues, since for these workers, physically separating the two becomes problematic. Over the past ten years, technology developments have led to the development of what is being called 'the remote work revolution'. Yet, if we continue to replace office-based work by fully remote work types, people's need for social interaction will still not be addressed. Some professions, such as programmers, are effectively trained to be independent remote workers. Yet other professions, especially those who need to build organic relationships with others, still need to work in an office.

The variety of challenges faced by young employees is not much different from what previous generations faced, but amplified by elements specific to the cyber age. One of the key challenges is that of maintaining a work-life balance. The findings of the latest Gallup State of the American Workplace report show that 43% of U.S. employees worked remotely in 2016, and in 2018 more than half of employees worked remotely 'some of the time'. On the one hand, there are positive effects on employee satisfaction and productivity. On the other hand, concerns relate to how remote workers are able to separate their work and personal life, remain coherent and engaged in working life, and build relationships at work.

CHAPTER 7

Impacts of Work-Life Balance on Job Satisfaction a

The traditional job structure has changed dramatically under the impact of the internet, as has the relationship between work and life. People always think, work, and even relax during both working and non-working hours. They have become accustomed to work without borders. With the outbreak of the COVID-19 pandemic, many organizations have been forced to quickly transition to a remote work situation, becoming accustomed to remote work, which may extend even after the pandemic. Researchers hold that organizations are paying more and more attention to work-life balance, which is not only conducive to improving employee job satisfaction, organizational commitment, and career success. In the information economy era, work not only needs to be done in the office but also can be completed with the help of technical means anytime and anywhere. Japanese scholars Akizuki and Idayu have carried out a longitudinal follow-up survey of Japanese telecommunications commercial employees. They found that the work performed outside the communication company using IT would help the staff reduce work-family conflicts and participate in family life more.

Work-life balance has been emphasized as an important aspect of employee physical and mental health. Modern people are struggling between personal life and work like never before. To achieve a good balance between work and life, both employees and employers should pay attention to it. Work-life balance is closely related to job satisfaction and job performance. On one hand, employees with poor work-life balance are less likely to be satisfied with their job. On the other hand, job satisfaction affects people's values, behaviors, and lives to some extent, which in turn affects job performance to a certain extent. Work-life balance and job satisfaction are important driving variables in the process of job performance. Researchers generally believe that the lack of balance between work and life will reduce job satisfaction and work enthusiasm, and reduce personal performance. A poor work-life balance may lead to poor working performance, even causing damage to the health of employees.

Research Findings

This section describes the underlying motivation for this research, the research framework, the survey instrument, the sample, and the response pattern.

The SparkPlace provides a very interesting and challenging environment for testing the research questions due to the emphasis they place on their employees who are spread all over the country. An entry to this new world paradigm is represented in Figure 1.1, a sweeping definition that includes both virtual work and remote work, as opposed to the narrow traditional scope that only mentions physical proximity. In the traditional sense, the term virtual work captures the combined meaning of telecommuting, teleworking, working from home, off-site working, etc. Companies in the midst of these changes are seeking to adapt workplace strategies by addressing telecommuting practices, deciding what technology should be in place to make it work, determining the best measurement procedure, etc. However, we feel the major start for business leaders is to understand the critical differences and the internal barriers to virtual work.

CHAPTER 8

Case Studies of Successful Work-Life Balance Imple

This chapter offers case studies of twelve organizations in the US, Europe, and Australia, which have successful work-life balance programs. They represent a variety of industries including high technology, business-to-consumer, manufacturing, finance, consumer goods, and government. The overriding factor of their success is that they act upon the belief that for a business to succeed in the long term, individual employees must also succeed. It should be of interest to scholars, managers, or practitioners interested in human-resource management, organizational behavior, and women's and family studies.

The new work-life balance: Succeeding in the remote work era seeks to produce a positive impact on employee work performance. Our belief is that a work environment can be created that is emotionally positive and respectful of personal time and still achieve business purposes. To accomplish this goal, case studies for organizations that have considered this "enhanced" work-life balance and have been successful were presented.

Company A

Company A offers complete flexibility in location, role, and project engagement. Employees have the ability to turn down assignments. Management and all employees choose their career path based on their own personal desires. The culture of the organization is truly that of "Can you help with this project?" Once the project has concluded, the employee returns to their personal metaphoric "salary protecting activities." This aspect of Company A allows a greater sense of work-life balance for all, regardless of if they have family care responsibilities. Company A also applies a start-up number of hours per week to their corporate job. There is less separation between business and personal life. The company values the ability to produce results with less effort. All employees are focused on completing the job. They are also very focused on clients and the quality of their work.

Company A exists in a completely virtual environment. There is no central, physical office, and HR, accounting, and other centralized functions are also outsourced. Employees have a work-at-home environment and access all proprietary systems via remote access. Tax laws and requirements are a concern due to lack of central office space and the location of the principal employees. Company A was formed via spin-off from a larger, traditional organization. It continues to share the marketing, legal, and other sales functions of the parent company.

CHAPTER 9

Future Trends and Predictions in Remote Work

If you're reading this, you know that communication through a screen has already proven itself an invaluable tool. The World Wide Web has allowed consumers and businesses to connect directly – offering goods and services from every corner of the globe, building business relationships with peers around the world, or reaching out through popular social media platforms. The future includes improvements in current tools in addition to greater experimentation and reinvention. Major technological shifts may challenge long-held beliefs and limitations, leading to breakthroughs in how work is completed. Tools like virtual reality, holographs, and artificial intelligence will enhance current remote work by increasing presence between team members and streamlining workloads.

Many of the industries that can embrace remote work have already begun moving their workforces into homes, co-working spaces, and local cafes. It's not uncommon to discuss business via text while soaking in a bath, play with baby goats on a farmhouse, or wear pajamas while transcribing.

In the next decade and a half, remote work will continue evolving as advancements and opportunities for both employers and employees are refined. Mobile office setups and fully remote teams will become the norm with the passing of each generation. While time will tell what tools and communication practices become the most widely embraced, it is clear that a talented virtual workforce can produce a great product at any time without a single person setting foot in a central office.

Technological Innovations

One of the biggest advantages of being able to work remotely is that it no longer matters where a firm's employees are located. This opens up great opportunities for companies and other organizations to truly leverage the vast quantity of talent that's located all around the world. Not being constrained by geography, firms can often achieve greater efficiencies by choosing the best employees to work with - no matter where they are located. This can lead to cost savings, but can also give firms access to a superior pool of diverse ideas, growing their competitive advantage over time.

Thanks to recent technological advancements, it's become much easier than ever for people to work together remotely. Collaborative online platforms like Git, Slack, Zoom, and others have made it easier for workers to work successfully together, no matter where they're located. The wide-scale introduction of new forms of artificial intelligence, which can automate various menial and routine tasks, frees up workers to focus on those more complex sorts of work where human intelligence really adds tremendous value.

CHAPTER 10

Conclusion

But work-life balance isn't like the scales of justice. You aren't trying to divide up your time so the scales are in perfect balance - it will never happen - there's always a little more on one side or the other. Work-life balance is your own recipe for juggling the important things in your life every day. When you set your priorities, you define your own balance - family, work, self, friends, and everything that's important in your life together in your perfect recipe. Covid-19 quickly remodeled many HR and business challenges. Remote work, schedules, location, and even the very tools of work itself were rapidly reexamined, scrutinized, and revamped. As your company fights to stay on top of its game in the modern business arena, look to the other areas of your operation, look to your policies and culture, look to your technology implementations, and look to your employees for help.

    Covid-19 has had an impact of epic proportions. It created rapid change for businesses of all types and sizes, but the remote work movement was not slowed down. Instead, it was accelerated. While there are and have been challenges with remote work, it has worked well for many, and people are looking at work differently now. No longer just "work", it's your day, your day-to-day, it's a vital part of life, and it has to be in balance with all the other important parts of life.

Key Takeaways

This new work-life balance is about the art of achieving priorities and trade-offs between many different parts of our life. As discussed above, many of us who work from home are learning or relearning our preferences, but there are some lessons that have emerged. With you mostly on Zoom video, we have to think deeply about how to manage our own engagement both to decrease too much attention to other subjects and to give everyone an incentive to be involved. We have been engaged in deeper connections with individuals with social distancing, increasing the need and making it easier to invest deeply in a few relationships. Finally, we cherish time away from our activities and have made us spend time with our loved ones. The new work-life balance suggests that success can be achieved during flexible working and that it always provides the best outcomes for the individual – the employee and the boss.

We are now working from home and will for longer than expected. Even as "shelter in place" rules are relaxed, it will take a long time for many office buildings to be full again, and the very nature of our physical and social worlds has changed. We will work from home more, use virtual formats for more of our interactions, and travel less. And work will continue. There will be more profound changes over time, but even short-term shifts create a need for new norms. This article has been about those changes. For leaders, who must support and set an example for their teams. For workers who must adjust. We've thought about striking balances in work demand, connection with others, and freedom from interaction. About how we constrain choice and how we manage the boundaries between work and home. We have focal points, and if we take them into account, we will achieve balance.